Life as I See It

By

Rich Tozzo

Disclaimer Page

Dedication

To my friends with which I have been truly blessed…

My Mom

She was born in 1923 and passed away three months shy of her 100th birthday. She was a hard worker around the house and preferred being home more than any other place, like a captain who never left the ship. Gardening and landscaping were her specialties and passions. Neighbors often complimented her as they passed by. Oddly, she never had a job.

After the divorce, she only socialized with her sister and closest friends. It's unclear why she never took a job; she never said, except to explain that she thought my father would help her. Not sure where she got that idea either. Nevertheless, she was a great mother who loved her children and grandchildren. She was beloved by all who knew her as a kind and cheerful soul. However, I had issues with her because in the last 20 years of her life, she made some serious life-altering mistakes. Despite any warnings from myself and my brother Howard, she continued to support my other brother William, who was 50 and capable of taking care of himself. These decisions had monumental effects. In the end, she lost her beautiful home and died virtually penniless.

My Father

He was also born in 1923 and died at the age of 88. He was a hard worker, as was his heritage, and was the first in his family to graduate college in 1950. He was able to buy a piece of land in North Haven, CT, in 1956 and built a fine home for us all. Despite his lack of patience, he was a good father. His attitude changed until 1968 when his own family became less important to him. I definitely had some issues with his life choices. Ironically, I was with him in Florida when he passed away. My mom was there too; she just happened to be visiting friends who lived in the general area. I distinctly remember my mother leaning over his bed as he was drawing his final breaths. "I'm leaving, Howard, going back to Connecticut," my mother explained.

He looked up and simply said, "Connecticut?" And that was his final word.

It gave me a lump in my throat that I was there to witness the final moments of a 70-year-long relationship. I was blessed to witness that.

This is a summary of my life and some of the events that shaped my future and made me who I am today. I could not write every event or name every person. If I did my story would make War and Peace, look like a short story. I truly hope you enjoy and get something out of it.

Contents

Chapter One 1

Chapter Two 18

Chapter Three 25

Chapter Four 30

Chapter Five 34

Chapter Six 41

Chapter Seven 51

Chapter Eight... 58

Chapter One
The Roots

"The Bible says, 'Honor your mother and father,' it doesn't say anything about liking them."

I was born in New Haven, Connecticut, in 1953. My father worked in the insurance industry, and my mother was a stay-at-home mom. We resided on the third floor of my grandparents' multi-family house. Despite my grandfather passing away in 1956, I still hold vivid memories of him. He was a loving presence in the lives of my brother, Howard, who was born in 1951, and me.

My grandfather, hailing from Italy, was a skilled cabinet maker, while my grandmother, Marion, was a seamstress. She immigrated to America at the age of 12 and had family connections in Stamford, Connecticut. The intriguing part is how my grandparents met; a detail lost to time. Together, they raised three children: David, Irma, and my mother, Saba, who happened to be the eldest. I cherished the close relationship I had with all my aunts and uncles; it was a true blessing.

In 1956, we moved to North Haven, Connecticut. My father often regaled us with a story from those early days in our new house. He recounted an incident when he was working on the roof, hearing footsteps behind him. To his amazement, he turned around to find me, a mere three years old, having climbed the ladder propped against the house. I was fearlessly wandering around, seemingly without a care in the world.

North Haven was a paradise for a child like me. When we initially moved there, our home was among the first to be built in the area. Marlen Drive, where we lived, formed a substantial circular layout, with a vast plot of undeveloped land nearby. I would often venture into those fields, discovering a world teeming with streams, brooks, and a myriad of wildlife. Rabbits, turtles, tortoises, and frogs abounded, offering endless fascination for an inquisitive youngster like myself.

In those bygone days, it was perfectly acceptable for a child to roam freely for hours on end without their parents' constant concern—though, in hindsight, perhaps not the safest practice. But that was the way things were for me. Beyond the confines of our property lay the Merritt Parkway, with a strip of land ripe for exploration. Additionally, there were three inviting ponds nearby, each brimming with fish, and catching those fish, as well as frogs, became a cherished pastime of mine.

I distinctly remember a day when I returned home with a net full of frogs I had caught. My father, upon seeing my catch, kindly instructed me to release them back into the wild, which I obediently did. There was even an occasion when I managed to capture a sizable snapping turtle and proudly brought it home for everyone to see.

I like to think of myself as a "free-range child" during those formative years. As I mentioned earlier, I would routinely venture out and be gone for hours on end, all the while, nobody at home would ever wonder where I had disappeared to. It was a time when such adventures were not only possible but also part of the fabric of childhood. One particularly memorable episode occurred when I was a mere five years old, and my older brother, Howard, aged seven, decided that we were going to run away from home. With determination, he set out on foot, and I, of course, dutifully followed his lead.

We managed to cover approximately half a mile before our adventure hit a roadblock. My father, showing up in the family car, intercepted our determined escape. He inquired of my older brother, Howard, about our destination, to which my brother confidently declared that we were running away from home. At my tender age, I hadn't quite grasped the significance of such an endeavor, but my father, with his characteristic wisdom, suggested that we return home and partake in a hearty breakfast before making any major decisions. A child psychiatrist in his own right, my father knew how to navigate such situations.

So, we relented and returned home to enjoy a meal before embarking on our journey once more. Our destination was my grandmother's house, nestled in Hamden, Connecticut, and a quick glance at modern mapping services like MapQuest reveals that it stood precisely 5.1 miles away from our residence in North Haven.

As we ascended the front steps of my grandparents' home, an uncanny coincidence unfolded. My grandfather, who worked just a few yards away across the street, was making his way back to his workplace as we arrived.

Meanwhile, my grandmother, Lena, swung the door open and was greeted by the sight of her two adventurous grandchildren. A look of concern crossed her face as she scanned the area and inquired about our parents' whereabouts.

It fell upon my brother, Howard, to explain our escapade. My grandmother promptly took action and called our home. My mother answered, and the conversation unfolded inquiring about our well-being. In response, my mother casually remarked that things were fine and that the kids were "around here somewhere." Little did she know that her "somewhere" was now miles away at her own parents' doorstep.

In the context of 1958, it's worth pondering whether such an incident raised any red flags. In today's world, it would certainly be a matter of concern, but in those more innocent times, it seemed that the freedom for a 5-year-old and a 7-year-old to venture out the door and wander for hours without constant supervision was, remarkably, not uncommon. The world, it seems, was a different place back then.

Speaking of 1958, it marked the first year we ventured down to Florida. Our mode of travel involved driving and bedding down in the back of our trusty Rambler station wagon. My father, a determined road warrior, would embark on this journey without any significant breaks, driving continuously from our home in Connecticut. It was a true adventure, particularly because there was no established highway system resembling today's I-95 back in 1958.

Instead, we navigated through a network of roads that wound through small towns, and as we ventured further south, the landscape grew increasingly rural, especially after passing through Washington, D.C.

During those long car rides, I distinctly recall seeing billboards dotting the roadside. These billboards served as advertisements for local restaurants and memberships to the Ku Klux Klan. Yes, you read that correctly. In those days, there were still blatant displays of racism, with signs indicating "restaurants for whites only" and even the presence of prison chain gangs.

Having witnessed these stark reminders of the racial divide, I can personally attest to the deeply entrenched racism that permeated certain parts of the United States during that era. It's a sobering memory that reminds me of the progress we've made as a society in addressing and challenging these injustices.

During the winter of 1958, we spent our time in Fort Pierce, and as luck would have it, my father had a friend who owned a hotel right on the waterfront. I can't help but wonder what that prime piece of real estate would be worth in today's dollars, in the year 2023. The hotel was known as the Palomino Hotel, and it left a lasting impression on me.

One vivid memory from that time stands out. I had a habit of rising early in the morning, a habit that persists to this day. On one particular morning, as the rest of the household was still nestled in slumber, I decided to venture out. I swung open the door to our room, and there, right on the welcome mat, lay a snake. Strangely, I had no fear of snakes, so I crouched down to get a closer look. Suddenly, seemingly out of nowhere, a burly man - everyone seems larger when you're just five years old - appeared and brought his work boot crashing down onto the snake's head.

As it turned out, this gentleman was the motel's maintenance worker, and the snake was no ordinary reptile; it was a genuine venomous rattlesnake. Believe me, had he not intervened, I would have likely attempted to handle the snake just a minute later. I shudder to think what might have happened had I been bitten by a rattlesnake in 1958. The outcome would likely not have been favorable. It truly felt as though divine intervention had sent that maintenance man at precisely the right moment.

I have another childhood memory from when I was quite young, probably no more than 5 or 6 years old. It was a day when we all went ice skating. While my parents could skate gracefully, I, on the other hand, hadn't quite mastered the art of skating. Instead, I contented myself with walking around on the icy surface, relishing the sensation of slipping and sliding on the frozen pond. This wasn't an indoor ice rink; it was a natural pond in another part of town.

As fate would have it, there was an unobstructed hole in the ice, and of course, my curiosity got the better of me. Despite being warned not to go anywhere near that hole, I couldn't resist. After all, it was just a hole in the ice, right? Well, as you might have guessed, I ventured too close, and before I knew it, I had plunged into the frigid water below.

I can't quite recall who it was, but someone nearby reacted swiftly and managed to grab hold of me, pulling me out of the icy abyss. Had it not been for their quick thinking and action, I might have gone under the ice, and that could have spelled the end for me as well. Of course it would have saved me 65 years of happiness and incredible pain. I can only imagine the panic and worry that this incident must have caused my parents; I'm sure it drove them crazy, especially my father who was not the most patient of men...

When I was 5 years old, everything seemed simple. But what can a 5-year-old really understand? My neighborhood was getting bigger, with lots more kids. This was during the Baby Boom, and two families moved in, each with 10 kids. That's 20 kids just from those two families! We all grew up together and played the usual kid games.

In 1958, my little brother William was born, and that changed our family a lot, pretty much for the rest of my life. William had some health problems that he still has today. So, my mom started giving him more attention, which makes sense because he needed it.

At first, I didn't really notice, but as the years went by, it became pretty clear to me. When you're a kid, you don't really think about your feelings or understand why you feel a certain way. But now that I look back, I guess I felt a bit left out. More attention for William meant less attention for me, and that didn't sit well with me as a kid.

As I got older, I noticed that my temper and my anger started to grow too. Generally, I was a shy but friendly and outgoing kid. However, I was also pretty scared of bullies. In middle school, if someone pushed me or knocked my books to the ground, I'd nervously pick up my books, hoping that the bully wouldn't do anything worse.

I wasn't a great student, but I really enjoyed science and history. I've had a love for animals that has stayed with me to this day. In fact, I had to repeat first grade, and they told me it was because I was born in November and too young at the time. I'm not sure if that's true, but I do know that I didn't do very well in school, especially in my first three years. It was confusing because I scored really well on the IQ tests, they gave us back then.

My struggles in school were so puzzling that my parents took me to a child psychologist to figure out what was wrong. Can you believe what they found? My eyesight was so bad that I couldn't see the blackboard or what the teacher was writing on it. It's kind of funny when you think about it. Mystery solved, but by then, the damage may have already been done. My early academic setbacks stuck with me for a long time, and so did my lack of confidence in my abilities. I used to think, "I'm not smart, so why bother?"

It wasn't until third grade that I got my first pair of eyeglasses. I still remember walking out of the eyeglass store and seeing the clock on the Hamden town hall for the first time. Without my glasses, I couldn't see the clock at all. I put my glasses on, and there it was, clear as day. That's when it hit me: this was probably why I couldn't see the baseball when I played little league. Even now, I can't help but smile when I see a young child, maybe 3 or 4 years old, wearing glasses.

As a child, I had no trouble heading off into the woods to try and shoot a bird or catch a frog with my bow and arrow or BB gun. I guess that's something kids often do around the age of 10 or so. But I would never even think about doing that now. These days, I enjoy hunting, but it's limited to wild hogs, and the meat I harvest is donated to a local food bank. The idea of harming a bird or any small animal is just not something I can imagine anymore.

In most cases, when I catch a fish today, I choose to release it back into the water.

By 1963, it was pretty clear that my dad was running out of patience. Instead of calmly advising me, he often resorted to shouting. It felt like he wanted me to mess up so he could tell me I was dumb. While he didn't hit us often, getting a smack on the head from him wasn't uncommon. One particular night my brother Bill was more annoying than usual and my father smacked him in the side of his head, knocking him to the floor. But I didn't mind too much because it meant his anger was directed elsewhere, at least for a while.

There's another memory that my family still talks about... It's the day I was late for dinner, which was a big no-no in our house. Dinner was always served at 5 pm sharp on weekdays, and missing it was a big deal. On this particular day, I had once again lost track of time while I was out exploring in the woods.

When I finally realized I was late, I hurried back home. From about 200 yards away, I could see my house, and I spotted my dad pulling the car out of the driveway. He was on a mission to find me. I watched as he drove slowly, looking left and right, trying to spot his late son. I knew he had seen me when the front of the car suddenly jolted forward as he hit the gas pedal, heading straight for me.

He pulled up to where I was and literally barked at me to get in the car. As we got closer to our driveway, he turned to me and said, "better run like hell when this car stops because I am going to kick your ass." True story!

As soon as the car stopped, I flung open the car door and sprinted away as fast as I could. I could hear my dad's footsteps right behind me. The good news is that I ran all the way around the whole house, and he couldn't catch me. Actually, he started laughing because he couldn't catch up to me. So, the crisis was averted. I guess I owe my dad a little thanks for helping me become a fast runner. In high school track, I ran the 40-yard dash in 4.9 seconds and the 100 meters in 10.6 seconds.

That was how things were in our family, and back then, I figured that's just how all families operated. I thought yelling was a normal way to talk. Even now, I'm not sure what he was always shouting about or why he never tried to change or calm down. But he was always upset or yelling about something, right up until the day he passed away at the age of 88.

By the mid-1960s, my dad was doing pretty well financially. He had a successful business and owned some rental properties. Around this time, he decided to get involved with the Big Brother organization. I'm not exactly sure why, given that he had three children, including me, whom he didn't pay much attention to. But I'm really glad he did.

Through Big Brothers, I met a boy named Vincent, who was about a year older than me. We became good friends, and he taught me a lot about how to be a man and how to stand up for myself, which was something I struggled with. See, I used to be really shy and afraid to assert myself.

Vinny had his share of problems too because he didn't have a dad. But not in the sense of getting into trouble. Like me, he didn't have someone to guide him through life. However, one thing he was drawn to was lifting weights. He was incredibly strong, and even today, 50 years later, I believe he still holds a record for the military press by a teenager, which was 300 pounds. I can't remember exactly but it was a record at that time.

Vinny and I used to hit the gym together, and we even entered weightlifting competitions all across New England. Thanks to Vinny's guidance, I transformed from the scrawny 90-pound weakling into a much beefier 190-pounder when I graduated high school. I went from being someone you could push around to someone you'd think twice about messing with.

When I look back at the bullies from school or summer camp, I wonder why I never went back there to settle the score. But honestly, it's probably for the best that I didn't. Instead, my confidence grew, and all that training eventually paid off. It made me a much better athlete and a stronger football player. So, a big thanks to Vincent for that.

Between the ages of 10 and 15, I formed my first real friendships, some of which I still have to this day. There are boys and girls from that time who I deeply care about and who are still part of my life now. One of those friends was a girl named Terry, and she ended up marrying a great guy I played football with in high school, Steve. Steve and I have been friends since 1966, and I even became the godfather of his only son. That's just one of the four godchildren I've been blessed to have in my life.

Many of the kids from our neighborhood grew up to be successful, outstanding individuals, and I'm proud to know them. In fact, most of them achieved more success than I did, but that doesn't bother me at all. They absolutely deserve their success.

When I entered middle school, I had to deal with bullies myself, which was tough. As I mentioned before, it affected me and probably contributed to some anger issues I had. These issues were both a curse and a blessing in my life.

I wasn't really scared of the bullies as much as I was embarrassed about being scared. I felt ashamed that I didn't stand up for myself. As I got older and started playing sports, particularly football, which I absolutely loved, I began to discover my own skills and strength.

I mentioned my friend Vinny earlier, who helped me grow both as a person and in terms of my physical strength through weightlifting. Back in 1968, weightlifting wasn't something most 14-year-olds were not into, but we were. When I started playing freshman football, I realized that hitting a ball carrier wasn't a problem, and knocking someone down didn't hurt at all. This is when my confidence really started to take root.

In 1968, my dad moved out because he was really into golf and other women, and he couldn't resist that call. He met his second wife at the country club and wanted to marry her. The problem was, she was not only not very bright but also already married. Back in those days, you couldn't get a divorce unless both people agreed to it. So, my mom refused to sign the papers for over two years, hoping he'd come back. And he did, every time he had a fight with dopey wife number two.

But it became clear that my dad wasn't coming back for good, so my mom eventually let him go so he could move on with his life. However, my mom didn't move on. She just stayed home as if she was still a housewife taking care of kids. She never got a job and didn't seem to think about the future or earning money. This has always puzzled me. Not getting remarried or even a boyfriend is one thing, but having no income and no plan for the future is incredibly confusing to me.

As for me, I didn't mind my dad being gone. It was actually a nice break. I was about 15, almost 16, and too big to be physically punished, but the yelling still continued. So, not having him around for that reason alone was a relief.

During the summer of 1968, I used to spend a few weeks at the shore with my aunts, uncle, and grandmother. It was a fantastic time, and I made friends with local kids who enjoyed swimming and fishing. But here's where I made my first big conscious mistake, not just a kid's silly blunder. I fell in love with a local girl, and thoughts of playing football went out the window. Once I returned to football training, all I wanted was to be back at the beach because, well, I was in love. It was a pretty foolish decision.

I quit the football team and hurried back to my grandmother's beach house as soon as I could. I've been kicking myself for that decision for a long time, although maybe I shouldn't be so hard on myself. While my friends were playing football and improving their skills, I was a bit foolishly hanging out at the beach. But as the months passed, I started feeling worse and worse about my decision.

My sophomore year in high school seemed to drag on, and my feelings for that girl lingered, which was to be expected. Then, at the end of my sophomore year, a football coach named Larry Cioti approached me. He said that I would be playing football in my senior year and that I'd be playing as a center. This is what I needed, someone to give me encouragement and that is what coach Ciotti did. I did in fact play center and defensive lineman in my Junior and Senior years. Oh my God if I only knew then what I know now. But probably most people feel that way.

In September 1971, I was a senior in high school, and honestly, I didn't have a care in the world. I had no idea what I was going to do in the future. But I felt fearless and was kind of a big deal on campus, especially with football season starting.

I enjoyed those last six months of high school. I didn't have a girlfriend, and I even skipped my senior prom because of it. But I still had no clue about what I was going to do after graduation. A friend suggested I go to preschool, so I gave it a shot. Unfortunately, it felt like a wasted year.

I should have joined the Navy and seen the world. Get some real-life experience even if I hated it. After 4 years, get on with something else. But I would have gotten Veteran benefits for the rest of my life. It is my single biggest regret.

In the summer of 1972, I met my future first wife. She was really attractive, and we got along great. However, our relationship had way too many ups and downs to be a serious one. Despite that, we both kept trying to make it work, which turned out to be another mistake. I'll tell you more about that later.

After high school, I went to St. Thomas More prep school and played football there, but honestly, I wasn't too keen on playing with a bunch of strangers. Looking back, I realize that now. I did make some friends, but they didn't compare to the ones I had in high school.

In the fall of 1973, I wasted another year of my life at the University of Rhode Island, although I wasn't entirely sure why. I felt lost. I didn't return for my second year and ended up bouncing between different jobs.

In 1975, I worked for my father at his insurance agency, and he paid me very little. But there was always something missing. It's funny how some people seem to know exactly what they want when it comes to school or a career. Even at the ripe old age of 22 I still didn't have a clue. I was still in an on-again, off-again relationship with my future wife during this time. I did the best I could working with my father but it was a struggle. Besided the fact that he expected me to work for virtually nothing, he wasn't any different as a boss as he was a father. To be honest, I was pretty lost, but I wasn't too concerned about it. Figuring everything would work out for the best.

One afternoon my father and I had a big fight over his girlfriend, and he ended up firing me. It came down to him choosing between me and her. Can you guess who he chose? Well, he chose her, and I was fine with that at the time. I left the agency and never looked back. I went home and drowned my sorrows in alcohol. I didn't speak to my father for about a year. What was the point, right?

But one day, my friend Vinny, who I was still close to, told me that my father needed to talk to me urgently. It was supposedly something important. So I drove over to see my father at a business he had a small interest in, only to find out that Vinny had made the whole story up. He just couldn't stand seeing a father and son not speaking. Vinny was a good man. And probably still is.

Leaving the agency was a turning point that forced me to think about what I was going to do next. I had a motorcycle and loved riding it, so I thought, why not get a job working on motorcycles? That's when I had my "Eureka" moment. I decided to go to a Trade School in Daytona Florida. Classes started in January 1977.

However I was out of work and in 1976, the job market was terrible, and I needed money. Motorcycle school was starting in January 1977. I went all over looking for work but there were no good jobs available. I drove out to a McDonalds in Orange CT but that position was filled. So, that manager suggested I try the McDonald's in West Haven instead. Off I went in my 1969 Volkswagen to apply there. I met the manager, and after a brief chat, he said, "Okay." This was in August 1976. I explained to him that I'd be leaving for trade school in January. He asked, "Then why should I hire you now?" I replied, "Because you can hire someone, and they might leave in a week. I'm giving you my word that I'll stay until January." He thought for a moment and said, "Alright, welcome aboard." And, in case you're wondering, I did stay until January, just as I promised. You see, a man, or woman, is only as good as their word.

It turned out to be a great job, really. Back then, McDonald's didn't serve breakfast. My day started at 6 am, and the manager had me cleaning the parking lot, emptying all the trash bins, and then burning the trash in our incinerator. It was quite neat. After that, I'd not only pick up litter on our property but the manager insisted I go one block down, pick up litter on that side of the street, cross the street, pick up litter on the other side, and then cross back over to the store. I have to say, the McDonald's I worked in was really amazing, and more specifically, the manager was one of a kind.

At 11 am, I'd head into the store and start cooking burgers and fries. And yes, before handling the food, I made sure to wash my hands thoroughly. I'd finish up around 2 pm and head home. It was a great job, and I'd recommend that every kid should work at McDonald's for a while. Sometimes, I wonder if I ever should have left?

Chapter Two
Highway Reflections

"If rivers and oceans and mountains can be overcome, anything made by man can be overcome."

I got to Daytona and completed the training I needed. and in the spring of 1977, I started my new job as a motorcycle mechanic. Man, was I nervous on that first day! But the team was so welcoming. One mechanic, Wayne, really went out of his way to help me out. We hit it off and became good friends. Even though he moved to another state and we haven't seen each other in 20 years, we still talk every few months. I'm really thankful for friends like him.

My confidence grew with time, and I started enjoying the job even more. Before long, I was promoted to service manager with a pay raise of $5.50 an hour, up from my starting wage of $3.50 in '77. Being able to talk with people and having a good understanding of mechanics made the role a good fit for me. I learned so much, and looking back, it's probably my favorite job ever. Doing what you love and having fun with it? There's nothing better. I definitely should have never left.

Things with my girlfriend were going well, and in August 1978, we decided to get married. The wedding day was nice, but a piece of advice for anyone: if you're getting married, tie the knot in the morning. We got married in the afternoon and by the time we got back to our hotel we overslept. We were so tired the next day we almost missed our ride to the airport. We had a great time on our honeymoon, first in Jamaica and then in Boston. Coming back to Connecticut, we began our life together in a condo, thanks to some help from my dad. It cost us about $36,000, and I remember stressing about how we'd handle the $280 monthly payments.

But life is full of ups and downs. I had some old habits from my past, like yelling and getting angry easily. This made things hard for my wife, I'm sure. Maybe I wasn't ready to be married or had some old issues I never dealt with. These things should be handled before getting married, not afterward. I never wanted to split up, but I think my wife might have felt differently at times. After every argument, I always felt bad. It's no excuse, but that's just how it was.

In 1979, a realization hit me: I needed to earn more. If my wife and I were to start a family, and she chose to stay home with the kids, I had to step up. I pondered my options, and after some thought, it came down to either becoming a welder or a truck driver. Truck driving won the toss. I committed my weekends for 4 months to truck driving school and obtained what was known as a Class 1 license, allowing me to drive big 18-wheelers. But there was a catch: when I began job hunting in 1980, nobody wanted a rookie. Today, companies are so in need of drivers that they'll hire and train beginners, but times were different then.

As luck would have it, I met a guy who leased trailers for big rigs. His offer was tempting – rent a trailer and start my own venture. There was just one hiccup: I needed a rig to haul the trailer. The solution? Purchase my own. I invested in an old, worn-out Mack truck. It wasn't the prettiest, but it was mine, and I was incredibly proud. While my wife wasn't thrilled about me being on the road for days at a stretch, I assured her that if the trucking life ever became too burdensome on our relationship, I'd hang up the keys. And I meant it.

With my truck and trailer sorted, the next step was finding cargo. I began scoping out local truck stops and gathering information. I chanced upon an ad for a broker in New Haven who needed loads delivered. He handed me my first assignment: transport goods from Springfield, MA, to Cleveland, OH.

Now, picture this: there I was, a newbie driving a massive rig to Springfield. What was going through my head? Honestly, not much. I was driven by sheer guts. I've heard as you age, you might become more cautious, but at 70, I still feel I've retained that youthful boldness. However, I marvel at my past self's audacity to dive into the trucking business headfirst.

The journey to Cleveland had its fair share of hiccups, like a minor issue with my trailer's brake lights, but I persevered. Mid-trip, I rang up my wife only to realize I had lost my voice – probably from the stress, which I hadn't fully acknowledged. Thankfully, I made it to Cleveland late that night, and the dockworkers, kind souls that they were, unloaded my cargo even though they were technically closed. Exhausted, I decided against finding another load for the return trip and drove straight home.

As time went on, the broker from New Haven and I developed a solid working relationship. He set me up with steady gigs, like transporting wire from Long Island to Ohio. I cultivated ties with other brokers, ensuring I always had a load to haul, whether I was heading out west or coming back east. One time, I even transported a batch of tires from Akron. Things were going well.

In April 1980, my wife expressed her wish to visit Florida with her parents. I hesitated initially – a parked truck doesn't generate income. But seeing how much it meant to her, I caved. I figured after a month of constant driving; a break would be good for me.

However, as life often shows us, a lot can change in the blink of an eye, let alone a month.

In the last week of February, as I cruised down Route 80 in Pennsylvania, a bizarre, unsettling feeling washed over me. It was a raw, chilling premonition of impending danger. Out of sheer instinct, I spoke aloud, addressing God, pleading, "Please, don't let me die. I've got so much left to see and do, and I want to be there for my kids." Then, during my return drive at dawn, with the sun peeking over the horizon, I felt a deep connection to the Christmas carol, "O Holy Night." When I sang the line "fall on your knees and hear the angels' voices," I was overcome with emotion and broke down crying. Months later, a minister suggested that this overwhelming feeling was the Holy Spirit touching me.

And as time has passed, my belief in that explanation has only deepened.

After that intense spiritual encounter in February, life resumed its usual rhythm. I got back from that journey, and nothing hinted that the weeks leading up to our planned Florida vacation would be anything out of the ordinary.

One of my jobs was to transport copper wire from Long Island – a good-paying, one-day trip to Ohio. After that delivery, my broker set up another load for me: 42,000 pounds of split green peas. I was told I wouldn't even have to oversee the loading. Pulling into the freight yard, I parked my truck and informed the loaders of the job. Deciding to catch a brief rest in my cab, I was soon interrupted by the feeling that something was amiss. Investigating, I found that in 20 minutes, they had only loaded 12 bags. The two loaders were painstakingly hauling these 100-pound bags, four at a time. My frustration erupted.

"STOP!" I yelled. "What's happening here?" Without waiting for their response, I phoned my broker and vented my frustration. After some back and forth, the broker posed the question: "Do you want the load or not?"

After a brief hesitation, I replied, "Fine, I'll take it, but don't expect to hear from me again." Frustrated but resigned, I instructed the loaders to continue.

Despite trying to rest while they finished, sleep eluded me. I don't recall the exact time I finally hit the road, but with a full load bound for Goya Foods, I was on my way. The day had been lucrative: $850 for the copper wire and another $450 for the peas. Nearing New Jersey around 11 PM, I pulled into a truck stop needing fuel. The lines were too long, so I decided to refuel the next morning. But come 6:30 AM, the situation was unchanged – long queues everywhere. So, I continued my journey along Route 80, searching for another truck stop.

Spotting one up ahead, I realized too late that it was on the opposite side of the highway. Undeterred, I decided to exit and cross over. But as soon as I took the off-ramp, I realized it was dangerously short.

Braking hard, time seemed to slow. I saw a school bus drive past and noticed a steep drop-off of about 60 feet ahead. "Well, I guess this is how it feels to die," I thought resignedly.

I hit the guardrail and felt myself dropping.

An indescribable peace enveloped me as I descended. If this was death, it felt serene. I remember thinking, "If this is death, I'll take it." The sound of metal crunching and tearing fairly filled the air, but fear was absent. Surprisingly, thoughts of my loved ones didn't come to mind, not my mom, my wife, or even my beloved dog. The soft rumble stooped.

Then, out of nowhere, I heard a voice shouting, "Are you okay in the truck?" That voice brought me back to the world of consciousness.

It was an odd sensation. First, I thought I must be dead. Then, I wondered if I was paralyzed because I couldn't feel anything below my waist. I remembered a movie about a world-class skier who broke her neck and couldn't walk again. I thought, what would I do if that happened to me? "Well, I guess I'm going to find out what that's like."

The voice soon had a face as a man peered through my passenger-side window. "I can't believe you're alive," he said. "And you won't believe the truck when you see it."

I fumbled for my wallet in my down vest pocket and handed it to him. "This is who I am. Call my brother Howard at his office." Five minutes later, he came back and said there was no answer. Of course, it was 7:05 AM. I then told him, "Okay, call my in-laws and let them inform my wife. I don't want her getting a call from the state police."

Next, it was time to get me out of the truck. The fire emergency crew had arrived, and they decided the best course of action was to slide me out the driver's side window. Bear in mind that I drove a cab-over tractor, and the cab was completely off the frame. I was lying on what used to be the windshield. The steering column hung right above me, and the emergency responders asked if I could grab it to pull myself up. "Sure," I thought. "My back might be broken, but my arms work just fine." At that moment, the pain hadn't set in yet, but I knew it was coming. As I pulled myself up, the emergency crew slid a stretcher under me, and out I came.

I was soon being rushed to Pocono Regional Hospital in an ambulance. My curiosity about the wreck was strong, but my instinct was stronger – I didn't want to see the mangled truck that had almost claimed my life. I shut my eyes, bracing for whatever was next.

Chapter Three
A Year of Transformation and Transition.

"Robert E. Lee said that when you go into battle, you must give it your all. Hold nothing back. You want it to be your last battle. The same I feel is true with any romantic relationship. Give it your all, hold nothing back."

On March 5, 1980, I found myself in the back of an ambulance, headed to a hospital I'd never been to, with an uncertain future ahead. Surprisingly, I wasn't anxious or worried at all. I had just experienced a profound religious moment, but it had slipped from my mind. I was fully awake and aware of my surroundings now. The memory of that peaceful darkness didn't return to me until sometime later.

When I reached the hospital, everything seemed hazy, but one thing was clear: the pain was intensifying. I requested a painkiller from my doctor, but he refused, insisting on identifying the source of my problem first. X-rays painted a grim picture, though it could have been even worse. One of my vertebrae was completely destroyed, vanished. I was then placed on an operating table, where I remained for a grueling 7-hour surgery.

The only reason they halted the surgery, as I later learned, was because my vital signs began to decline. The surgeon I was fortunate to have had served in Vietnam and had encountered numerous spinal cord injuries. I believe he was still in the naval reserve, as I distinctly remember him visiting me in his full uniform once. He took the time to explain the extent of the damage and confirmed that I indeed had spinal cord damage. However, the silver lining was that most of the nerve damage was peripheral and had the potential to regenerate over time. It was a waiting game. He went on to mention that the orthopedic surgeon had considered a spinal fusion, but my weakened state wouldn't permit it. The fusion would have to be a future endeavor.

During that time, my wife, my father, my in-laws, and everyone else made the journey to Pennsylvania to visit me. They were all deeply concerned, but I tried to reassure them not to be overly worried. I genuinely held onto the belief that I would recover and be okay.

Ten days later, I was transported back to New Haven, Connecticut, to Yale New Haven Hospital. There, I would spend the next 60 days following my final surgery. Once again, I was fortunate to have a remarkable surgeon,
Dr. Bradburn, who was a part of the New Haven Orthopedic Group. He personally conducted the entire procedure, from the initial incision to the final suture. He inserted steel rods and used bone from my hip to stabilize the affected area. Remarkably, I haven't experienced even the slightest ache or pain from that surgery in over 40 years.

I experienced pain in other places, but surprisingly, not in the surgical area. Additionally, I was placed in a cast that extended from my arms to my waist. For weeks, I wasn't allowed to sit up. Instead, they placed me on a special bed that rotated me like a ham every four hours. I had to eat while lying flat on my back or flat on my stomach. It's incredible what you can adapt to when you're left with no other choice. The striker bed was designed to prevent pressure sores, which is why they rotated me regularly.

I managed to make it all the way back to my home in Wallingford, Connecticut, on a Sunday in May 1980. I'm fairly certain it was Mother's Day. Everyone came over, and we had a sort of celebration, though looking back, it probably wasn't the best idea. Nevertheless, I was back in my own space, sleeping in a hospital bed in our living room.

We lived in a townhouse with the bedrooms upstairs. So we had a hospital bed but in the living room. Could not use my legs so crawling up the stairs was my only option. Never will forget my first shower or bath after I had my body cast removed. The best things in life are free and that was an incredible experience for me. I'd lost about 20 pounds and was able to lift myself in and out of the tub. Plus I'd always been strong and my arms were more than capable. My physical therapist Rita was wonderful and she helped me understand the issues I was about to face. Spinal cord injuries affect your limps but, in my case, also my bowels and my bladder. Had to wear a diaper and as you can well imagine how that affected my pride. Naturally it affected my wife as she was not a nurse. Thus is not what she signed up for. It affected my recuperating abilities in my opinion. It stopped focusing on the task at hand. I learned from my mother's cousin Ray about the power of positive thinking. Ray had throat cancer and the outlook was bleak for him. But he started reading books by Ernest Holmes. Basically explaining that your body can heal itself but it has to have a positive outlook. More importantly your mind has to have a positive outlook. So I'd repeat countless times "I am in perfect health, I am in perfect health". Whatever positive thoughts I could muster I'd run them over and over again. My boyhood heroes we. General Patton, Vince Lombardi, and Billy Martin. I watched the movie Patton so many times I adopted his Opening speech. Made it my own. When Patton said the soldiers under his command would "wade into the enemy: I made my disability the enemy. When Patton spoke of advancing "Constantly" I was advancing Constantly. One inch a day no matter how far, you will get there. Just advance Constantly. I live by the words of Ernest Holmes and general Patton to this very day. Is it easy? Hell no. But when you stay focused, remember to move that inch every day, it can be done. In any endeavor you decide to take up. And my ability to stand on my own, to walk on my own, was my only goal. That may not be 100% accurate. As my other very important goal was to be able to have sex again. Most if not all men would probably be in that same boat. I'm blessed with a great imagination, or is it a curse I could fantasize about having sex again. To help me along, my good friend Wayne, motorcycle shop Wayne, who I mentioned earlier, brought me a stack of playboy and hustler magazines. That was a big help. Lol. I was not going through life with a, pardon the expression. "Limp dick".

I'm happy to report that the area of my recovery came about faster than my legs. Now through all this my relationship with my darling bride got worse. Found out she was seeing a co-worker so I decided to go to Florida and continue my rehabilitation. It went well and for 3 months I made steady progress. Was able to stand on my own and walk using 2 crutches. Not bad. Returned to Connecticut and my wife moved out shortly thereafter. I Continued to improve and even was able to drive myself around. Joined the local YMCA and started an exercise group at 6 am. God forbid you came in late. "You're late: I would bark. "This is not a cruise ship"! But it was all good-natured fun. Shortly after that my good friend Dave opened a gym. That's when my progress really took off. Everything that worked got bigger and stronger. When you exercise correctly it has too.

Chapter Four

Graduating to the Next Phase of Life

"One can move two but two can move ten. Remember this if and when you are married."

In September 1981 I went back to college. I went to a local community college and received a 2 year Associate's degree. Then I went to Quinnipiac College for my next 2 years and graduated in 1985 with a degree in Financial Management. I wanted to work in the investment field. Like a stock broker. But after graduating, I applied to multiple stock brokers for a position, but my lack of experience seemed to be a deal-breaker for all of them. That led me to travel to Washington DC, where I stayed with some close friends, Steve and his wife Maureen. Stayed for approximately 6 months. My time there was incredible—I fell in love with the city and had some unforgettable Saint Patrick's Day celebrations. The experiences were so remarkable that I feel they could fill another book.

When searching for work in Washington DC, it became evident that while there were numerous job opportunities, there were just as many recent graduates vying for those positions. Thankfully, my friend Steve helped me secure a temporary job in a lab. However, after spending three months at that job, I made the decision to return to Connecticut.

In 1983 I won a lawsuit against the Great state of Pennsylvania. It seemed like a lot of money at the time but it was no were near enough for what I went through. But the state had a maximum limit they would be responsible to pay if they lost a lawsuit. So in 1985, fortunately, I wasn't in dire need of money, but I was eager to dive back into work. I took up jobs in Connecticut with different life insurance companies, but none really captured my interest. That's when I made the decision to venture into entrepreneurship. After thorough research, I settled on the idea of launching a Pak Mail mailing center. The prospect excited me, and everyone I discussed it with seemed to think it was a fantastic idea. I underwent a two-week training session in Denver, and after several months of meticulous preparation, I finally opened my store in 1990.

Things were going relatively well, and I found enjoyment in running the business. My main competitor, Mail Box etc., closed down after a year or two, leaving me in a favorable position. My store was situated in Meriden, Connecticut, nestled in a lovely shopping center—a choice guided by Pak Mail's business recommendations. However, as you know, a prime location comes with a hefty price tag. Over time, the rent became increasingly burdensome, particularly during slower months. Then, my landlord declared bankruptcy, presenting what seemed like an opportunity to renegotiate the lease. Unfortunately, the new landlord wasn't open to discussion, prompting me to hire a lawyer just to secure a few more months. In hindsight, it was a costly mistake.

I developed close relationships with some of my customers and felt a sense of responsibility toward them. However, in 1993, I made the difficult decision to close down the business and face the consequences.

As I mentioned earlier, my time at Pak Mail introduced me to some remarkable individuals, and with some, I developed strong bonds. I even fell in love with a couple of them. What's amusing is that both relationships flourished. We connected well and genuinely enjoyed each other's company. One of them, a few years after my Pak Mail days, expressed the desire to marry me. I won't disclose her name, but I was head over heels in love with her. The thought of spending every day with her for the rest of my life filled me with immense excitement. Imagining her smiling face as I drifted off to sleep each night and waking up to that perfect face every morning brought me immense joy.

For me, that marked the conclusion of our story. I was getting married and my thoughts and concerns were for us and our future. We used to attend church together on Sundays, and she mentioned her desire to get baptized in the Spring of 1993. I was completely supportive of the idea. Sadly, it didn't materialize. However, the silver lining is that I experienced a spiritual rebirth that spring and became a born-again Christian. I vividly recall driving to the church alone, hoping she would join me. I sat there, gazing at the door, eagerly waiting for her, wishing she'd fulfill the promise she made months earlier. Waiting for the door to open and for her to walk in and sit by my side. Romantic dope, yes?

But, as fate would have it, she never showed up. When my turn for baptism arrived, I descended into what felt more like a hot tub than a baptismal font. Under the water I went, and the minister recited, "I baptize you in the Father, the Son, and the Holy Ghost." As I emerged from the water, unexpectedly, laughter burst out of me. I couldn't quite explain it, except that it was a laughter born out of the overwhelming joy I felt in that moment.

The overwhelming emotions I experienced were incredible. I had an impulse to drive to my loved one's home, but I realized she might not believe me if I shared my feelings. She could have thought it was merely a ploy to see her again. If by chance she reads this, she might recognize herself and perhaps understand the depth of my feelings for her. Yet, if she truly knows me, she's already aware of that.

One thing I've realized about being born again is that after the initial elation, a sense of sadness creeps in. You become attuned to certain undeniable truths that you can no longer ignore.

Coming to terms with the realization that some of your deeply held beliefs aren't valid isn't an easy journey to navigate. Jesus being the way and the truth—that truth can indeed sting. It's disquieting to see oneself in a different light. The growth that follows after baptism takes time—months, even years. It's akin to planting a seed or a young tree. You witness its growth and observe the changes, yet there won't be any fruit from that tree for years to come. Moreover, without proper nurturing and care, the fruit that eventually sprouts may be of poor quality, or worse, there might not be any fruit at all.

"I'd give everything I own for one happy marriage."

- J. Paul Getty

Chapter Five

Real Estate Romance and New Beginnings

"If you could kick the person in the pants responsible for most of your trouble, you would not be able to sit for a month."

- Theodore Roosevelt

In 1993, after what I can only describe as a personal rebirth, I found myself pondering my next steps, uncertain of the path ahead. The loss of my Pak Mail store had left a gaping financial void, with my bank account echoing its emptiness. Scrambling for solutions, I managed to sell some equipment from the now-shuttered store, which brought in a modest but crucial lifeline.

In these trying times, my friends, as they often had, became my anchors. Their support materialized in the most practical form – work. My foray into the working world began with installing tile for a friend's carpet and tile installation business. Though I considered my contributions modest, the opportunity was a much-needed stepping stone. Once again, a friend saves my ass.

One Saturday, driven by nostalgia and perhaps fate, I decided to visit my old boss, Bob Miller. Bob had been the owner of the motorcycle shop where I first worked. He had since transitioned to a custom motorcycle chop shop in Clinton, CT. It had been over a decade since our paths had crossed, but our reunion unfolded into a long, heartfelt conversation. A few days later, to my surprise, Bob called with a job offer. It wasn't as a mechanic but to manage his parts inventory. Gratefully, I accepted, likening myself to a drowning man unconcerned with the hue of his lifeboat. Being around motorcycles again, immersed in their mechanical symphony, and having a purpose each day was rejuvenating. Once again, a friend had extended a helping hand in my hour of need.

And there's more to say about Bob Miller. After I left the motorcycle shop in 1980, I believed I had lost my health insurance – a trivial expense less than $20 a month. Unbeknownst to me, Bob continued to pay for it. This act of kindness revealed its true magnitude in March 1980, when I suffered an accident. Without that insurance, I shudder to think where I would have been. This single act paints a vivid picture of the man Bob Miller was.

As the summer of 1993 waned, my financial situation gradually stabilized, allowing me to breathe a little easier. Opportunity knocked again when I applied for a manager position at a Circle K store. The offer came just before Thanksgiving, a timely blessing. The job was good, the pay reasonable, and I was responsible for the first shift, from 7 am to 3 pm. The store, open round-the-clock, was manned by other employees during the remaining hours.
This routine continued seamlessly for almost a year. The 45-minute drive to work each morning became my sanctuary, a time for reflection. Financially, things were looking up, but I was still living paycheck to paycheck.

Then one morning, in a candid conversation with God, I expressed my financial woes. Speaking aloud, I half-jokingly pleaded for a mere $10,000 to ease my burdens. The very next day, in a twist that seemed like divine intervention,

I checked my bank balance. The automated voice informed me that my balance was $10,700. I was dumbfounded. It was the exact amount I had asked for. Initially, I thought to wait, unsure of this unexpected windfall. When I checked again, the balance remained the same. I resolved to use the money if it was still there the following day. However, as luck would have it, my balance had returned to its original $700. A subsequent apology letter from the bank revealed the $10,000 deposit had been an error. Nevertheless, the coincidence was uncanny – a fleeting glimpse of what could have been, and a humorous reminder of life's unpredictability.

After a year at Circle K, I felt an itch for something more, a yearning to be my own boss again. The desire to embark on a new venture was palpable, but it had to be something manageable, something that didn't demand a colossal investment. Then, like a lightbulb moment, it struck me: becoming a real estate agent. It was perfect. The autonomy to come and go as I pleased, the effort I put in directly shaping my success.

With determination, I delved into studying and preparing for my realtor exam. The joy and relief I felt upon passing it were immense. Now the question arose: where to work? The school where I had learned about real estate laws and practices also ran a real estate company and offered me a position, but I chose a different path. I joined a Century 21 office in North Branford, CT. The first two years were a whirlwind of making contacts and closing sales, a testament to my dedication.

However, just as I was settling in, the realtor who owned the office decided to close it. Almost serendipitously, at that moment, my phone rang. It was my old teachers, now extending an invitation to join their firm. The timing was impeccable. It was an ERA Real Estate office, and fortuitously, they were opening an office in my hometown, North Haven. Real estate, I had come to realize, is deceptively simple, which perhaps explains why so many diverse individuals find success in it. It boils down to meeting people, forging connections with loan officers, and essentially, just talking to people. Everyone either owns a house or aspires to own one.

Our new office in North Haven adopted a unique approach. We designated a day solely for phone outreach. All the realtors would gather, phones in hand, ready to dial. It was straightforward: dial, talk, connect. Our office had an extensive phone directory, and I would often pick a street in a desirable neighborhood and start calling.

My approach was direct, no frills, no catchy phrases. When someone answered, I'd simply introduce myself: "Hi, this is Rich Tozzo with ERA Fort Hale Real Estate here in North Haven. I was just calling to see if you had any interest in buying or selling any real estate now or in the near future?" This simplicity, this direct human connection, was the crux of my approach. It was about reaching out, establishing a rapport, and understanding people's needs and dreams. In this new chapter of my life, I was not just selling houses; I was helping people find homes, a mission that brought a profound sense of fulfillment and purpose.

In the realm of real estate, responses to cold calls were as varied as the colors of autumn leaves. From outright rejections and stern 'drop deads' to curious inquiries about property values. But regardless of the reply, I maintained my composure, offering thanks and moving to the next number with undeterred enthusiasm. The key, I learned, was in the persistence, the firm resolve to continue calling. Every 'no' simply meant that I was one call closer to a 'yes'. This principle wasn't just limited to real estate; it was a universal truth in the world of sales. The mantra was clear: never stop calling, stay positive, and don't quit.

This period of my life also brought about an unexpected twist. One day, while waiting for Chinese food to take back to the office, I stumbled upon a magazine featuring single women from around the globe. Out of curiosity, I browsed through it and, on a whim, decided to send a letter to one of the women listed, facilitated by a $5 fee from the magazine. It was a small decision, seemingly insignificant at the time, but as life often proves, even the smallest decisions can lead to substantial consequences.

In response, I received a letter from Maria in the Philippines. She was pleasant but expressed no interest in me or in coming to America. I respected her decision and moved on. However, a few months after Maria stopped writing, I received another letter, this time from Esmeralda, a friend of Maria's. Esmeralda expressed interest in writing to me since Maria was no longer in the picture. Little did I know that this exchange would eventually lead to her becoming my wife. It was a testament to how life's paths are shaped by seemingly inconsequential choices.

Meanwhile, my career at ERA Real Estate was flourishing. I had the honor of receiving two sales awards, and as a single person with minimal responsibilities, it felt like the perfect career choice. A fruitful connection with a mortgage broker opened doors to several clients, particularly those looking for their first homes. While first-time buyers often gravitated towards more affordable properties, the satisfaction of helping them find their first home was immensely rewarding. The effort required to close a $100,000 deal was no different from a $500,000 one, but the joy and gratitude of first-time homeowners were incomparable. It was a heartwarming experience, witnessing their dreams materialize into reality, a tangible space they could call their own. In these moments, I realized that real estate was not just about transactions; it was about creating lifelong memories and fulfilling dreams.

The year 1997 marked a period of stability and contentment in my life. The condo I had owned since my marriage, now a rental property, provided a steady stream of supplemental income. Meanwhile, my correspondence with Esmeralda continued to blossom. Letter writing, an art often forgotten in the digital age, became our bridge across continents. There's a unique intimacy in penning letters, a way to convey thoughts and emotions that sometimes get lost in the immediacy of modern communication. For me, this old-fashioned method of staying connected brought us closer in ways I hadn't anticipated.

Esmeralda and I grew increasingly fond of each other through our weekly letters and phone calls. Our bond, forged through words and voice, was strong enough that we decided to meet in person. In the fall of 1998, I embarked on a 26-hour journey to the Philippines, a trip I deemed well worth the effort. The two weeks we spent together in the Philippines were nothing short of magical. We explored historical sites, immersing ourselves in the rich drapery of Filipino culture. The country's beauty was matched only by the resilience and tenacity of its people, who had bravely fought for their independence and proved to be invaluable allies in World War II.

Despite the economic challenges faced by many in the Philippines, there was a prevailing spirit of hard work and determination, qualities embodied by Esmeralda herself. Our time together solidified our feelings, and we decided to get married. Esmeralda made the journey to America in September 1999, and we began a new chapter of our lives together.

Adjusting to life in America was a unique experience for Esmeralda. She was younger than I but carried a maturity that belied her years. We initially stayed with my mother, a decision made to ensure Esmeralda would have company and support while I was at work. This arrangement also provided a period of adjustment and acclimatization for her.

In November 1999, Esmeralda and I tied the knot, and shortly thereafter, we moved into our own apartment, marking the dawn of the new millennium with new beginnings. Our relationship, born from letters and nurtured across miles, had taken a significant leap. It was a time of hope, of looking forward to building a life together, and of embracing the uncertainties and possibilities that lay ahead. The year 2000 promised a fresh start, not just for us as a couple, but in every aspect of life, filled with opportunities and challenges alike.

"By all means, marry. If you get a good wife, you'll become happy; if you get a bad one, you'll become a philosopher."

- Socrates

Chapter Six

*Bittersweet Journey Through Love,
Liberation, and Self-Discovery*

*"I'm for the truth no matter who speaks it. I'm for
justice no matter who it is for."*

- Malcolm X

In November 1999, as the new millennium's dawn was about to break, Esmeralda and I embarked on a journey together as newlyweds, filled with hope and dreams. We settled into our own apartment, a tangible testament to our commitment and the fresh beginnings that lay before us. However, the journey was not without its twists and turns, testing our resolve and adaptability in ways we hadn't anticipated.

Our first major decision was to get a place of our own, a cozy nook that symbolized our union. Life in our new abode was mostly serene, marked by small joys and shared dreams. Esmeralda, with her nurturing spirit, chose not to work initially, dedicating her time to making our house a home. Meanwhile, I took a decisive step in my career by joining Metlife. This decision, I later realized, was a misstep considering the flourishing state of my real-estate career. The allure of a job with regular hours and benefits was strong, yet the reality was far from my expectations. It was not the conventional 9-to-5 role I had envisioned; instead, it often involved long days and even longer nights, stretching my limits and testing my patience.

Amidst these professional challenges, we reached another milestone: Esmeralda obtained her driver's license, and together, we bought a car. This newfound mobility was a symbol of our growing independence and adaptability. Esmeralda's innate love for children led her to a fulfilling role at a local daycare center. She flourished there, her maternal instincts making her a favorite among the children. To support her family back in the Philippines, she also took a part-time job at a supermarket, diligently saving to send money home.

Sending money to the Philippines soon became a recurring theme in our lives. Our commitment to support Esmeralda's family was firm, yet it sometimes strained our resources. I vividly recall an instance when we sent $2,500 to cover her mother's hospital bills, an event that made me question the veracity of the situation. Was her mother really detained in the hospital until the bill was paid, or were we just being taken advantage of? These doubts occasionally clouded my mind, yet I continued to support them, hoping our efforts were genuinely helping.

I often pondered the sustainability of this financial support. One evening, I voiced my concerns to Esmeralda, "What happens when we can no longer afford to send money? Will they ever be in a position to help us in return?" Her response, or lack thereof, was disheartening. It seemed she either couldn't grasp the gravity of the situation or chose not to, perhaps bound by a sense of duty and love for her family that transcended financial practicalities.

As the years rolled by, our life together continued to evolve, shaped by our choices, sacrifices, and the unspoken promises we made to each other. The journey was far from smooth, but it was ours - filled with love, learning, and the occasional leap into the unknown. And as we navigated through these challenges, our bond, though occasionally tested, grew stronger, a testament to our commitment to each other and the life we were building together.

As our marriage journeyed through a decade, the road was often rocky, with challenges both seen and unseen. Looking back, I realize that over those ten years, we had sent nearly $20,000 to the Philippines. My focus was on immediate responsibilities, failing to see that Esmeralda, perhaps, never envisioned a long-term future with me. The year 2002 emerged as the most turbulent in our marriage, a year that retrospectively, should have marked its end.

Our routines were simple yet distinct; I frequented the YMCA in the mornings, while Esmeralda preferred the afternoons. It was during one of these routine days that an unexpected phone call pierced the ordinary – a man asking for Esmeralda. He left his number for her to call back, a number I withheld, yet secretly kept. A feeling of unease nestled in my heart, leading me to unearth the address linked to that mysterious number.

Weeks passed, and on a quiet Saturday night, with curiosity and dread as my companions, I drove to the address. The sight of Esmeralda's car parked outside the house at 9:30 PM sent a chill down my spine. My heart was heavy with apprehension, yet I chose to wait. After thirty minutes, I mustered the courage to knock. The man, hesitant and evasive, never fully opened the door, but Esmeralda did appear. It was clear; she had met someone at the YMCA, and the nature of their meeting was no longer just my imagination.

Driving back home, I called the number, asking to speak to Esmeralda. When she came on the line, I simply advised, "Do not come home tonight." She agreed, but about an hour later, she was at our doorstep, creating a scene loud enough to stir the neighborhood. She claimed she was leaving and began to pack. In response, I drove aimlessly for hours, lost in a haze of smoke and confusion.

Returning home to find her asleep, I quietly packed my belongings and left for my mother's house. In my heart, I had concluded that our marriage was over. However, days later, Esmeralda reached out, pleading for forgiveness. She insisted that nothing significant had happened and that I was the only man for her. Her words, although persuasive, echoed with hollow assurances.

Standing at this crossroad, I was about to make one of my gravest decisions. Against my better judgment, I chose to forgive her and continue our marriage. This decision, laden with hope but devoid of foresight, would later reveal itself as a profound mistake. It was a choice that would shape the years to come, a lesson in love, trust, and the complex web of decisions that bind us.

The year 2002, a period marked by trials and turbulence, saw Esmeralda and I navigating through a multitude of challenges, both in our personal lives and our careers. Esmeralda, despite having a circle of hardworking and loving Filipino friends, seemed to gravitate towards individuals who were less than honorable. Perhaps, in their company, she found a sense of belonging that justified her own actions. I'm no psychologist, but I often pondered over her choices and their implications on our life together.

Professionally, the year started on a rocky note for me. After leaving MetLife, I found myself struggling to find a fulfilling job. A brief stint in car sales yielded predictable and unsatisfying results, further straining our already precarious marital situation. However, as summer approached, a ray of hope emerges. In August 2002, I landed a job at Herbasway, a company specializing in liquid green tea and other health products. The role in sales was exhilarating; our phones rang incessantly following our nationwide radio infomercials. This job not only brought financial stability but also a sense of accomplishment and fun.

Esmeralda, meanwhile, continued to juggle her full-time job and the part-time position at the supermarket. I remember rushing home from work just to drive her to her job, cherishing those brief moments together. Gradually, as 2002 drew to a close, our financial woes eased, and we began to save money. The shadows of early 2002 seemed to recede into the background.

The calm, however, was short-lived. In the winter of 2002-2003, Esmeralda met with an accident. An icy morning, a loss of control, and her Chrysler Sebring convertible was wrecked. Thankfully, she was unharmed, but we were now in need of a new car. We settled on another Sebring, this time in gold, and life continued its unpredictable march.

The year 2003 was relatively uneventful until August when we embarked on a memorable journey. My father, celebrating his 80th birthday, hosted a grand party in Florida, inviting family and friends. Esmeralda, my mother, brother, and I made the trip from Connecticut in a rented Cadillac, a journey marked by bonding and reminiscences. During this visit, my father, running a small insurance agency, proposed that I move to Florida to help him. Despite my inner voice cautioning against it, the prospect of a change was tempting. My current job was good, yet the history of business dealings with my father was a mixed bag at best.

But change was in the air, and the allure of a fresh start, coupled with familial obligation, nudged me towards what I now see as a misguided decision. It was a choice that would redefine our lives in ways I couldn't have foreseen, a leap into an uncertain future driven by the hope of betterment and the undercurrents of unresolved past dynamics.

September 2003 marked the beginning of a new chapter for Esmeralda and me as we packed our lives into boxes and set off for Florida. The optimism of a fresh start was palpable, yet overshadowed by an unspoken truth: simply moving doesn't erase problems unless you also leave behind old habits and mistakes. This was a lesson my 15-year-old niece, Jessica, had imparted years before, when she ended a relationship with her boyfriend was caught cheating on her. I asked why she broke it off and she simply stated, "because leopards can't change their spots." Her words, echoing wisdom beyond her years, resonated with a truth I had failed to heed.

Upon arriving in Florida, we temporarily lived with my father, a situation that was manageable but fraught with challenges. My father's insurance agency, small and struggling, barely generated income. With no knowledge of the Florida insurance market, I found it difficult to drum up new business. Meanwhile, Esmeralda found employment at a shoe store, a job that seemed to suit her perfectly. Our daily routine revolved around a single car, with me driving her to and from work, a routine that I found surprisingly comforting.

In 2004, we achieved a semblance of independence by purchasing a condo on a picturesque lake, situated on the fourth floor and fully furnished. This move, a significant step towards establishing our own space, was marred only by my dwindling income. The Florida insurance landscape was boisterous, further aggravated by Hurricane Charlie and subsequent storms that struck within our first year. The homeowners insurance market was in disarray; companies were exiting the state or outright refusing new business. This left me in a precarious position, struggling to find viable insurance options to offer.

These challenges led me to question the very decision to move. Why had I left a job I loved in Connecticut to venture into this uncertainty? What had prompted my father to invite me to join his struggling business? Deep down, I knew collaborating with my father was risky, yet I proceeded, driven perhaps by familial obligation or the allure of change. But as time passed, it became increasingly apparent that his motivations were more self-serving than altruistic. I was caught in a situation where I had foreseen the pitfalls but had chosen to walk into them regardless, a decision that now left me grappling with professional stagnation and a sense of personal betrayal.

The year 2005 brought a significant change: the closure of the small insurance agency in Coral Springs, Florida. The venture, despite earnest efforts, proved unsustainable. This closure led me to a nomadic professional life, working at various small insurance agencies until 2007.

It was a period marked by uncertainty and the relentless pursuit of stability.

During these rowdy times, Esmeralda and I maintained a semblance of harmony. The shadow of her past infidelity seemed to have receded, or so I believed. In 2007, a new opportunity arose with Universal Property, a small insurance company. This job was a breath of fresh air, providing not only consistent work but also a relaxed and enjoyable environment. I met great people there, and for the first time in years, I felt a sense of professional contentment.

Esmeralda, too, was thriving in her career. Her dedication and sales acumen were evident, although, much like before, a significant portion of her earnings was sent back to the Philippines. This financial commitment, while noble, often left me pondering the balance between familial duty and our own financial security.

2008, however, reopened old wounds. The adage about the leopard and its spots rang true once more. Esmeralda, through her interactions at work, became close to a colleague who expressed more than a professional interest in her. My suspicions, unfortunately, were confirmed one Saturday night when I stumbled upon her emails. The messages detailed plans for a weekend getaway, complete with concocted excuses for her absence. The pain of betrayal, though familiar, was no less poignant. Confronting her yielded the usual denials, but the truth was too glaring to be obscured by feeble excuses.

In December of that year, seeking a respite from the turmoil, I decided to visit my brother Howard and my sister-in-law Martha in Texas. Their company, along with the joy of being around my nephews, always brought me a sense of peace and normalcy. The visit was not just a break from the routine; it was a necessary escape from the emotional upheaval back home. In the warmth of my family's presence, I found a temporary solace, a reminder of the uncomplicated love and support that family can provide. It was a much-needed balm for my troubled heart, a momentary haven from the storm that was my marriage.

My journey back to Florida, after a brief but soothing stay in Texas, was marked by introspection and a newfound clarity. The open road has always been a place of solace for me, a space where thoughts and decisions seem to crystallize. During this drive, a call from Esmeralda interrupted my reverie. She inquired if I had received her email, which I hadn't, and then revealed her desire for me to extend my stay in Texas. By then, I was already halfway back to Florida, and turning around didn't seem feasible. This conversation lingered in my mind, and in the early hours outside Orlando, a realization struck me: if Esmeralda wanted the marriage to end, it would be on my terms, not hers. I decided then that I wouldn't be the one to leave; if she wanted out, she would have to make the move.

To my surprise, she stayed a few months longer, but the inevitability of our separation was clear. Early in 2009, Esmeralda found her own apartment and moved out while I was at work. The image of her moving over a hundred pairs of shoes bought a wry smile to my face. The logistics of that move must have been something to behold.

The legal dissolution of our marriage came in April 2010, with Esmeralda taking care of the formalities and court costs. Despite the end of our marriage, we occasionally saw each other, a relationship based purely on fleeting moments of pleasure. This arrangement, devoid of emotional strings, seemed ironically perfect in its simplicity.

But in all seriousness, the finalization of our divorce was a profound relief. The moment she walked out of my life, it felt like a heavy burden had been lifted. The constant stress of wondering about her whereabouts and actions was gone. She could have pursued any path, even as extreme as pole dancing, and it would not have mattered to me anymore. My only regret was not having the courage to end things sooner. Should have given her the boot in 2002.

Reflecting on this boisterous chapter of my life, I realized the importance of listening to one's instincts and the value of self-worth. The end of our marriage was not just the conclusion of a troubled relationship; it was the beginning of a new chapter in my life, one filled with possibilities and freed from the shadows of doubt and betrayal. It was a time to rebuild, to rediscover peace, and to embrace the future with a renewed sense of optimism and self-assurance.

"A chain is only as strong as its strongest link. That goes for people too."

Chapter Seven
Embracing Freedom

"If you don't love your job, find one you do."

In April 2010, I finally felt the weight of the past lift off my shoulders. The legal dissolution of our marriage brought an unexpected sense of liberation, and I couldn't help but echo the sentiments of Martin Luther King Jr.: "Free at last, free at last, thank God almighty I'm free at last." Surprisingly, Esmeralda and I found ourselves navigating the post-divorce landscape amicably. Our interactions were marked by a newfound civility, a pleasant departure from the unrestrained days of our marriage. Esmeralda, once my spouse and now my ex-wife, remained surprisingly kind and considerate, even going so far as to stop by occasionally. It was a curious turn of events that left me contemplating the enigmatic nature of human relationships. Perhaps the shared freedom from the chains of matrimony allowed us to rediscover a semblance of friendship.

Life continued within the confines of the condo; a residence still held in Esmeralda's name. In a peculiar arrangement, I paid her rent, creating a scenario that appeared unconventional but strangely functional. The dynamics of our post-divorce relationship defied societal norms, yet it worked for both of us. The condo, nestled by the serene shores of a lake, provided me with a comfortable abode, and in return, Esmeralda received a reliable source of income. It was a win-win situation, where financial pragmatism prevailed over emotional entanglements. As the waves lapped against the lakeshore, I found solace in the arrangement, living in a beautiful space at a fraction of the cost I would have incurred elsewhere.

The unconventional nature of our post-divorce life prompted introspection. I pondered the essence of freedom—freedom from a failed marriage, freedom to forge an uncharted path, and freedom to redefine the boundaries of relationships. The condo became a symbolic haven, a place where the complexities of our past dissolved into the tranquility of the present. Amidst the ebb and flow of lake waters, I discovered a sense of balance in this unorthodox coexistence.

Navigating the intricacies of our arrangement, I couldn't help but marvel at the irony of it all. While our marriage had crumbled under the weight of emotional discord, the aftermath brought forth a peculiar harmony, a delicate dance of mutual benefit. The financial pragmatism of our arrangement allowed me to savor the luxuries of lakeside living, while Esmeralda found a practical solution to her housing quandaries.

As I embraced the freedom that came with the end of our marital ties, I also embraced the uncertainty of this new chapter. The condo on the lake, once a symbol of marital unity, now stood as a testament to the resilience of unconventional connections. The arrangement allowed me to rebuild not just my life, but also my understanding of relationships. It was a time of reflection, adaptation, and the slow realization that life's narrative can take unexpected turns, leading to uncharted territories filled with both challenges and opportunities.

In the wake of divorce, I discovered that liberation came not only from severing ties but also from redefining them on my own terms. The condo on the lake, a place where echoes of our past lingered, became a canvas for a new beginning. The tranquility of the waters mirrored the newfound peace within, and as I gazed across the lake, I couldn't help but feel a sense of gratitude for the freedom that allowed me to sculpt my own destiny.

As the echoes of freedom resonated in the walls of the lakeside condo, life had one more unexpected twist in store. A hurdle, unforeseen and formidable, emerged in April 2011, casting a shadow over the newfound sense of liberation. My legs, already burdened with limited sensation, became the battleground for a fierce and silent war.

It began innocently enough—an infection in my left foot. Underestimating its severity, I attempted to self-treat, only to watch helplessly as it spread to the right foot. In a state of urgency, I sought help at a local hospital, where the initial attempts to address the issue proved inadequate. The infection, cleared by intravenous antibiotics, had left a silent trail in the dead tissues and bones, biding its time.

By July, the right ankle remained swollen, a persistent reminder of a misdiagnosed and mistreated condition. Esmeralda, despite the complexities of our past, stepped in as an ally. Together, we sought expertise beyond the local confines and found ourselves on a journey to the renowned Cleveland Clinic. Despite their expertise, the verdict was grim—they suggested heading to the University of Miami hospital, known for handling such complex cases.

In a moment of solitary determination, I drove myself to Miami, my hope resting on the possibility of saving my foot. The reality, however, was stark. The doctor, after an MRI, painted a grim picture—saving the foot meant sacrificing a significant portion of its bones, leading to a prolonged period of wheelchair confinement lasting six to eight months.

Faced with a difficult decision, I weighed the options, contemplating the trade-off between saving a part of me and regaining mobility sooner. In the end, I chose the path of amputation, anticipating a swift recovery with the aid of a prosthetic foot. Little did I know that the road ahead was paved with challenges far beyond my expectations.

The amputation plunged me into a world of uncertainty, far removed from the anticipated ease of a prosthetic solution. A month in a wheelchair felt like an eternity before the prosthetic foot could be fitted. When the moment finally arrived, the reality struck hard—I was weak, unsteady, and vulnerable, akin to a kitten taking its first steps. Daily exercises became my regimen, a testament to resilience and determination. Slowly but steadily, I reclaimed the ability to move, though the truth remained undeniable—a prosthetic could never truly replace the intricate craftsmanship of the human foot, a creation deemed irreplaceable by the divine.

In the throes of this physical battle, a profound realization dawned—the strength to endure, to adapt, and to persevere was not solely rooted in the physical realm. It emanated from a steadfast spirit, an acknowledgment that the essence of resilience transcends the limitations of the body. As I grappled with the challenges of my altered reality, the belief in the indomitable human spirit became my guiding light, propelling me forward into the uncharted territory that lay beyond.

April 2013 marked a significant turning point as I bid farewell to my role at Universal Insurance. In a decision tinged with regret, I chose to return to the familiar embrace of Connecticut. However, the pull of Florida was relentless, and by September 2013, I found myself contemplating a return to the Sunshine State, with the hope of securing a job offer from MetLife.

The prospect of a position at MetLife was enticing, promising a potential permanent return to Florida. During the interview process, a curveball emerged—I was asked if I'd be willing to relocate to North Carolina in two years. Without hesitation, I affirmed my flexibility. The interview concluded with one last question, a seemingly innocuous inquiry about the number of hires they were seeking. The response, "30," lingered in the air.

As I drove back to Florida, a nagging thought took root—maybe I wouldn't be the top choice, but surely, I wouldn't be the last. A week later, reality hit hard as I received the unexpected news that I was, in fact, candidate number 31. The initial disappointment gave way to a realization—a twist of fate had intervened. Perhaps, in the grand scheme of things, there was a divine plan at play.

In the aftermath of this revelation, I reflected on the unexpected turns life had taken. While the MetLife opportunity slipped through my fingers, it became apparent that there was a larger force guiding my path. The decision to stay in Florida, once again, seemed like a nod from destiny. It was a realization that sometimes the plans we make are mere outlines, subject to the whims of a higher design.

In the end, the words echoed by Jesus, the wisdom of a higher source, proved prescient. Despite the setbacks, I found peace in the unexpected twists and turns that kept me anchored in Florida. As I embraced the unfolding narrative, I recognized that every detour, every disappointment, was a thread woven into the fabric of my life—a fabric that continued to reveal its intricate design, one chapter at a time.

During my stint in Connecticut, an unexpected arrangement unfolded, symbolizing a peculiar yet harmonious phase in my life. Esmeralda's parents took residence in the apartment, creating a very agreeable living situation. Their presence brought a sense of familial warmth, and I found comfort in knowing that all but one of my feathered companions were in good hands. Lucky, the African Grey parrot, accompanied me on the journey, while the other three avian companions enjoyed all the attention bestowed upon them by Esmeralda's parents.

The timing of my return to Florida coincided with a pivotal moment—Esmeralda loading her SUV and embarking on a journey northward. The subtle yet profound shift in our lives was palpable, as the physical distance mirrored the emotional separation that had taken root over the years. It was a tacit acknowledgment that our paths had diverged, and the ties that once bound us had loosened.

As I settled back into the rhythm of Florida life, I reflected on the trajectory of my journey. The separation from my ex-wife, marked by geographical distances and newfound independence, served as the exclamation point to the end of our 15-year relationship. The minutes of our first separation had initiated a positive trajectory in my life, and each passing day brought incremental improvements. The move to another state became a symbolic punctuation mark, underscoring the evolution and transformation that had defined this chapter of transition.

Remarkably, the absence of Esmeralda from my daily life became a source of liberation. The burdens that once weighed heavy had gradually dissipated, replaced by a sense of autonomy and self-discovery. The separation had become a catalyst for personal growth and an opportunity to redefine the contours of my existence.

In the aftermath of our physical and emotional parting, I found solace in the present moment. The echoes of our past had faded, and the specter of our former life together no longer loomed over me. The journey forward unfolded with a sense of clarity and purpose, free from the entanglements of a relationship that had run its course.

As the chapters of my life continued to unfold, the separation served as an emotional reminder that closure, however it manifests, paves the way for new beginnings. The expanse of time and distance between us became a canvas upon which I painted a new narrative—one filled with resilience, self-discovery, and the promise of a future unburdened by the shadows of the past.

"Many a battle has been lost because the army stopped on the wrong side of the river."

Chapter Eight

What Now?

"Do what you can, with what you have, where you are."

"Believe you can and you're halfway there."

"It is hard to fail, but it is worse never to have tried to succeed."

- Theodore "Teddy" Roosevelt

The last 10 years have been fun but rather uneventful. Working various jobs in the insurance industry. Bought a condo and sold it to buy another. I started hunting wild hogs here in south Florida, as they are a real nuisance. Also did more fishing going on guided trips into the everglades and in any of the 1,000s of places here in Florida. I even managed to get back on the road. Buying a Harley trike which allowed me to ride a motorcycle again.

Most of my friends are woman but romance continues to allude me. The only steady female relationship is with a woman currently in prison. I saw her story on a true crime drama and my heart went out to her feeling her sentence was unjust.

I wrote her over 3 years ago and we've been writing ever since. I've even visited her twice in Pennsylvania. She means a lot to me. It's ironic that the best relationship I've had with a woman over the last 15 years is one that I cannot do anything about.

As I look back on the past 70 years, I've realized that life is a mix of exciting, tough, thrilling, and challenging moments. What stands out to me is that life is all about choices. Sometimes, I've made decisions that didn't turn out so well, and other times, a small choice led to a huge, life-changing event.

I've learned that even the smallest decisions matter. Like that one morning when I didn't fill up my gas tank the night before. If I had, I wouldn't have been looking for fuel at 7 am. Instead, I would've gone straight to Goya Foods and probably been safe and sound at home that very day. But because I didn't get gas earlier, things took a different turn.

It's surprising how a seemingly insignificant decision like not filling up the tank could impact the course of events. It's made me realize that life is unpredictable, and even the smallest choices can lead to big consequences.

Looking back on the last 70 years of my life, I've come to accept that if it wasn't the accident on March 5, 1980, something else might have happened later on – maybe in April or July, or at some other time.

I've begun to believe that there was a bigger plan at play. All the difficult experiences I faced as a child, like falling through the ice or getting my hand caught in the clothes ringer at age 3, seem like they were preparing me for something bigger that I had to face later in life.

It's as if those tough times were shaping me for the challenges that were yet to come. Looking back, it feels like everything that happened was somehow connected, almost like it was all part of a plan to help me endure whatever was ahead in my life.

Looking back, I realize that every person I met and every event I experienced played a role in preparing me for a particular day.

I remember feeling more spiritually aware just a week before it happened. Then came that day when I had a near-death experience. Somehow, I managed to stay positive even after facing such a terrifying moment.

Thinking about it now, it seems like no matter which career path I chose, something challenging was going to happen to me eventually. It's like all those experiences and encounters were getting me ready for that specific moment in time.

What I've learned is how crucial it is to appreciate what you have. It's so easy to overlook things because, well, that's just how we humans are. We rush through our days, like spending only five minutes in the shower. I remember a time when I could get ready and be out the door in just five minutes if needed. Back then, I didn't appreciate my first wife enough. Looking back, I realize I didn't understand her value then.

It's a common human thing, isn't it? Not fully realizing what we have until it's too late. If you're in a relationship with someone you deeply care about, it's important to express that and cherish every moment. Instead of worrying about the future, focusing on doing your best each day is what matters. Appreciate having someone to share your life with.

This reminds me of a movie I saw from 1940. It was about a young William Holden who marries his high school sweetheart. They have a beautiful life together, but sadly, she passes away during childbirth. The movie portrays her spirit going back to relive moments from her childhood, like when her mother made breakfast and the delightful smell of fresh coffee and baked bread filled the air. It taught me the importance of treasuring the simple, everyday moments we often take for granted.

The movie scene where the woman longs to express her feelings to her mother, realizing the beauty of life only after facing a near-death experience, struck a chord with me. It made me think about how often we fail to appreciate the greatness of life while we're actually living it. The relief when she wakes up alive, holding her newborn, is such a powerful moment.

Reflecting on relationships, I've learned that they're not easy. It takes effort, patience, and understanding from both partners. Being on the same page is crucial—understanding what you like and dislike about each other. It's the dislikes that can strain a relationship. When everything is fun and enjoyable, it's easy, but what happens when tough times hit? Like losing a job or facing financial struggles? Those moments test the relationship, but what I've learned is that holding on and being patient is key. Things can get better over time.

There's a quote by J Paul Getty that resonates with me: he said he'd give up everything he had for just one happy marriage. It emphasizes the value of choosing wisely and staying committed during both the good and challenging times in a relationship.

It's important to be in sync with your partner in a relationship, but never give up on your own beliefs and values for the sake of harmony. I've experienced those times when everything seems okay and then suddenly it's not. What I've learned is that it's crucial to listen to your heart and stick to what you believe is right, something I didn't always do in the past.

Looking back, I realize that I'm here at this moment because of the choices I made. I didn't always follow my instincts or do what felt right to me, and that led me to where I am now. It's a reminder to trust my own feelings and intuition more often in life.

Where I am right now is a result of all the choices I've made. Even if I took advice that turned out to be not so great, ultimately, I made the decision to follow that advice.

That's just how life works.

I hope sharing my experiences might help someone else see things in a similar way. It's important to appreciate what you have, especially a loving spouse and children if you're fortunate enough to have them. Time flies by, especially as we grow older. Life seems to speed up, just like how the roll of toilet paper goes faster as it nears its end.

The main point is to value and cherish the people and moments that matter most, because time doesn't wait for anyone.

We never really know when our last day will come. It's important to find happiness and feel blessed, even during tough times, no matter how hard they may seem. My dad used to tell me something like, "Stop crying or I'll give you something to cry about," and now imagine God saying that. It's a way of emphasizing that we should appreciate what we have and not dwell too much on our difficulties.

The point is, there's always someone who might be going through something tougher than us. It's a reminder to be grateful for what we have and try to find contentment in our lives, even when things are challenging.

"The only true wisdom is in knowing you know nothing."